Moments With Massy ® series is dedicated to my a
I especially want to thank my granddaughter Adrienne, who
the beginning to the end of this relatable and entertaining story
Additionally, I want to thank the incredible educational profes............ .. .. Elementary
School in Fremont, Ohio for the countless opportunities to witness their unwavering commitment
to each and every student.

Kellie Carte-Sears

New School!
How Cool!

Written by
Kellie Carte-Sears

Illustrated by
Anahit Aleksanyan

Copyright/Legal Page information:

Moments with Massy ® Social Emotional Learning book series.
New School! How Cool! ©
Carte-Sears, Kellie

New School! How Cool! /written by Kellie Carte-Sears ; illustrated by Anahit Aleksanyan
Publisher Sears Enterprises LLC

Summary: Since Massy just moved to a new home, she is now faced with fears of riding a new bus and going to a new school. As her mom helps her get ready the night before her first day of school, something unexpected happens. Her lovable cat Blue sneaks into her backpack and secretly travels on this adventure with her.

Interest age level: 03-10.

1.Change-Juvenile fiction. Moving, New School 2.Household Juvenile fiction. 3.Adjustment (Psychology) in children-Juvenile fiction. 4.Moving, New School Household-Fiction. 5.Change-Fiction. 6.Adjustment (Psychology)-Fiction

First published by:
Sears Enterprises LLC Fremont, Ohio

Printed in the United States of America.

I'm so happy for you, Massy!
Tomorrow's your BIG day!
You start a brand new school-
An adventure's on the way!

You may feel a little stressed,
and perhaps you're even scared,
but here is my advice -
It helps to be prepared.

Pack some paper and some pencils-
Everyone needs those;
and put some tissues in your backpack -
You may need to wipe your nose.

Take your scented markers
and your favorite plushy, too.
These things will bring you comfort
if you start feeling blue.

Lay your clothes out neatly;
find your shoes the night before.
Put your backpack where you'll find it,
right beside the door.

You'll need to wake up early,
So, Massy, don't forget -
Before you go to sleep,
your alarm clock must be set.

Now, Massy, go to bed -
and get a good night's rest.

Ssssshhhhh.

I must be quiet -
(At least, I'll do my best!)

Wake up! Wake up!
It's morning!
Your adventure has begun.
You are fearless. You are brave.
Your new school will be fun!

Brush your teeth
and comb your hair,
wash your face, get dressed.
Eat a healthy breakfast, too,
is something I suggest.

The bus is parked out front
with the stop sign on display.
Greet your driver, find a seat,
then you'll be on your way.

You see new faces all around-
friends you haven't met.
Just smile and be yourself.
You'll make new friends, I'll bet.

Some kids look kind of sleepy.
Some kids laugh and grin.
Some speak with an accent.
Some have different skin.

Some kids in the back
seem to make a lot of noise,
but what can you expect
with so many girls and boys?!

Look! You have arrived at school.
It seemed a very short ride!
It's okay if you're nervous.
It's time to go inside.

A counselor takes you to your class.
It's nicely decorated!
Your teacher put a lot of effort
in the room that she created.

There are posters on the wall,
and a comfy reading nook
with a big soft rug to lie on
as you read your favorite book.

Oh, my! There is a hamster.
Teacher says her name's Nanette.
The children take turns feeding
their beloved classroom pet.

Teacher welcomes
all the children
when the bell rings
long and loud.
The students scramble
to their seats.
It's such a happy crowd!

"One, Two, Three, all eyes on me!"
That's the teacher's way
to make sure the children listen
to what she has to say.

Then teacher says very clear
for all the class to hear:
"We have a brand new student;
WELCOME MASSY
with a cheer!"

She assigns a friend to help you
until your first day's over.
She shows you all around -
Your new friend's name is Clover.

For math, you play a game.

Who knew math could be such fun?!

It helps you practice adding.

Your teacher says, "Well done!"

Soon you go to reading groups
where you can learn some more.
You read and learn
some words
that you didn't know before.

It's already time for lunch!
What do you have to eat?
A cheese and pickle sandwich,
and an apple, juicy sweet.

Some children want to sit with you
so you don't have to eat alone.
You meet Ava, Moe, and Cindy,
Joe, and Carlos, and Antone.

Yay! It's time for recess.
What fun to play outside!
Oh no! Moe's tooth fell out
as he was *swooshing*
down the slide!

The children gather 'round to see.
"That's awesome, Moe!" they say.
"The tooth fairy's going to visit you;
today's your lucky day!"

Next the children all take turns
at skipping rope or swinging,
but they must go back in
when the recess bell starts ringing.

It's time to learn some science. The children watch a show about different kinds of weather and what causes wind to *blow*.

Then teacher brings out paints
of every shade and hue.
How did she know that art
is your favorite thing to do?!

Quickly the day has ended!
The buses line up on parade.
Pack your things and say goodbye
to all the friends you've made.

Soon the bus has dropped you off
right at your front door.
That's when
you notice something
that you had not seen before!

Yes! I've been in your backpack—
a handy place to hide.
Just in case you needed me,
I was by your side!

"Massy, I'm so proud of you!
Your first day was successful!
You learned a lot and
made new friends -
It was hardly even stressful!"

That's because you were prepared,
and your attitude was cheerful.
That's the proper way to face
the things that make us fearful.

ABOUT AUTHOR

YEARS AGO, when KELLIE CARTE-SEARS learned her young grandchildren were moving to a different city from where she lived, she decided the best way to assist them with this change was to find a book that would help them embrace their emotions and let them know everything would be okay- a book that would show them moving didn't have to be so scary but could be fun and adventurous.

But she couldn't find a book that was "real" in a way that her grandchildren would personally connect. So Kellie went home and wrote her first book and Best Seller *"Moving Away Will Be Okay"*, the first book in the **Social Emotional Learning book series**, **Moments With Massy** ®. Today her books sell worldwide and continue to earn stellar reviews and top ten seller rankings.

An entrepreneur for over 30 years, Kellie Carte-Sears started businesses as a way to solve problems. Her drive to fulfill market gaps and the needs of others has gained her remarkable success on many different platforms.

Her newest book series, **Moments with Massy**® is no different. An advocate for education, she has a Bachelor's degree in Business Administration, Associate of Arts in both Social and Behavioral Science and Psychology, is a Trustee at a State College, and is a Substitute Teacher.

Using her experiences, education, insights, and the gifts God has given her, she is offering her books as a way to assist children and families during changes, challenges, and new opportunities.

Word Search, Color Pages, and other FREE games:
MomentsWithMassy.com/fun

Hope you had fun reading the book! ♥

Ratings are important,
it would be kind of you-
to take a brief moment,
and post a review!

(On Amazon and/or Good Reads)

Like and Follow
Moments With Massy® on

○ instagram.com/moments_with_massy/

f facebook.com/MomentsWithMassy

Made in the USA
Monee, IL
28 October 2024

68879115R00026